The Litt[illegible] u

Cather[illegible]

In association with the Réunion des Musées Nationaux

KATE'ART EDITIONS

In the time of

In the late 1800s, people went from place to place on horseback, in horse-drawn carriages and on foot. The streets were busy! Goods such as coal, flour and wine were transported from the countryside to cities by boat and by cart.

Henri Rousseau

With the new century came new inventions, including the first cars and airplanes. Ocean-going steamships replaced sailing vessels. With the new telegraph and telephone, people could send instant messages and talk over long distances. And electricity was invented too!

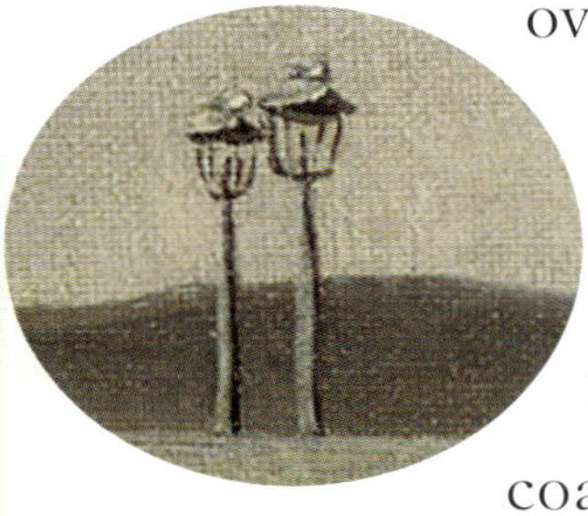

Homes were lit with oil lamps and heated with coal. Each evening, lamplighters lit the gas lights that lined the city streets.

People traveled to far away places in Africa and Asia. Many of them brought home exotic plants and animals.

Henri Rousseau

Hello! My name is Henri Rousseau. I was born on May 21, 1844 in a small town in France called Laval. I have a brother and three sisters. My father was an artisan and fine metal-worker. I was not a very good student but I loved to draw and make music. After finishing school, I studied law for a while. Then I accidentally got mixed up in a petty theft. To avoid problems with the police, I joined the army.

All my life, I have dreamed of far away places, but I have never left France. My life is so ordinary. To make it seem more exciting, I have led people to believe that I have gone on exciting expeditions in dark forests and fought in the Mexican War. The stories I tell my friends and acquaintances make me dream even more.

Draw a far away place from your dreams.

Giant Artist

Who is this giant who towers above everything? He must be an artist since he is wearing a beret and holding a palette. And he must be very important since he is so big compared to everything else in the picture. It is the artist, Henri Rousseau.

Rousseau painted himself larger than life. You can see Paris behind him. He wanted to be the greatest painter in France and he dreamed of becoming famous like his friends, Paul Gauguin and Pablo Picasso.

Can you find these details in the painting?

Flags

The Eiffel Tower

Hot Air Balloon

Beret

Carousel Bridge

Quay

Paint Brush

Chimneys

Artist's Palette

Customs Inspector

When he was 25, Henri Rousseau married Clémence Boitard. Three years later, they moved to Paris. Clemence helped pay the rent by working as a seamstress. Henri got a job as a customs inspector.

What are these customs inspectors doing?

Rousseau worked for over 20 years at the outskirts of Paris and in the ports along the Seine. His job was to see what goods were coming into the city and collect a tax on them – goods such as salt, milk, and oil. His job was boring, but he needed to work to provide for his growing family. Often, while his coworkers passed the time playing cards, Henri looked out at the landscape. He was fascinated by the forms and colors he saw. He once said, "When I see this sun, these flowers, I say to myself, "All of this is mine."

Create your own landscape in the style of Henri Rousseau. Look closely at his forms and colors.

Paris

Rousseau loved Paris. At first, he painted what he saw around him: the customs house where he worked, the bridges over the river, and other Paris scenes. His boss even gave him permission to paint during work hours when business was slow. He liked to paint everyday life and special celebrations. He was also very patriotic and painted scenes that honored France.

Rousseau painted scenes of the city: the Eiffel Tower, Notre Dame cathedral, and the city's bridges across the Seine. In his paintings, Rousseau depicted a city filled with calm, not the busy and bustling boulevards of real life. Rousseau's streets are nearly empty and time seems to stand still. Soon he began to visit the Louvre Museum to copy great masterpieces there.

What do you think the lone man is feeling as he looks out on the quiet city?

Naïve Artist

When he was nearly 40 years old, Henri decided to be an artist. He spent his Sundays and days off painting. Rousseau never took an art lesson. He taught himself to paint and developed his own unique style.

Rousseau knew he was a great painter. He never doubted his talent. But others called his paintings "primitive." They thought he drew like a child. The people and objects he painted looked flat, without perspective. Everyone faced forward and was strongly outlined. He used uniform blocks of colors, without any shading. And yet, his paintings had a mystery to them.

Which of these hands looks most realistic to you?

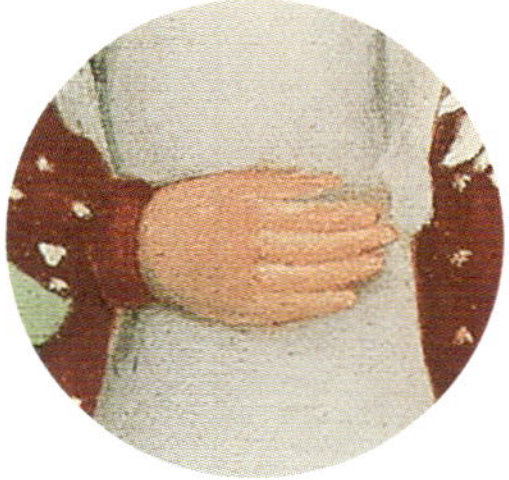

Botanical Gardens

Henri loved nature, plants, and animals. When he had a day off from work, he would go on long walks in the country. One thing he loved to do more than anything else was to visit the Botanical Gardens in Paris. He especially loved the greenhouses filled with exotic plants. There he felt as if he were in a different world. He saw plants that came from far away lands, and he imagined that he too was far away, in the heart of a tropical forest.

Henri Rousseau once said, "When I am in the greenhouses and see the exotic plants, I feel as if I am in a dream." When he returned from the Botanical Gardens, Rousseau set about painting jungle scenes. He greatly enlarged the plants he had seen, turning them into magical forests.

Can you find these plants in Rousseau's jungle paintings?

Reeds

Cactus

Eucalyptus

Agave Plants

Oranges

Snake Plant

Ferns

Palm Trees

Lotus Blossoms

Green

Rousseau loved the color green. He used many different shades of it in his paintings. On his walks in the country and in Paris parks, he collected leaves and branches. Their colors and shapes inspired him when he painted his jungle scenes.

How many shades of green can you find in the painting?

Color these leaves with different kinds of green.

Wide-Eyed Tiger

In the deep tropical forest, lightning strikes! The trees and grasses sway as the wind howls through the jungle. The sky is dark. All the animals have taken shelter. Even the fierce tiger is surprised by the booming thunder. He hides in the tall grasses. Is he scared?

After five years painting scenes of Paris life, Rousseau began creating jungle scenes from his imagination. He used the plants he'd gathered on walks and seen at the Botanical Gardens, and pictures in natural history books, to create paintings filled with mysterious and exotic creatures.

Make up a story about the wide-eyed tiger.

The Snake Charmer

Beside a wide river, by the light of the full moon, Yadwigha, the snake charmer, plays her flute. A snake is draped around her neck. Under the spell of her music, the jungle animals come closer. Who are the inhabitants of the mysterious forest?

How many snakes can you find in the painting?

Are those branches or snakes in the trees? It's hard to tell what's a snake and what's a branch in the dense and dark jungle. The snake charmer looks out at us, transfixing us with her gaze.

Which of these animals are listening to the snake charmer?

Dog

Snake

Lion

Tiger

Monkey

Bird

Cat

Crow

Owl

Jungle

The wild animals are timid. They hide in the foliage, camouflaged by the leaves. The jungle is filled with noises. Parrots, monkeys, snakes and other wild creatures screech and call to one another. Many wild eyes are watching us!

What animals can you find hiding in the jungle?

Which of these details does not belong in this painting?

Wild Beasts

Watch out! The jungle is filled with danger as different animals fight to survive – predators eating prey. Lions, tigers, jaguars, snakes and monkeys. Who will attack? Who will be eaten?

Rousseau never saw a real jungle. He created his jungle scenes from his imagination. He got ideas for his paintings from his visits to the zoo and the museum of natural history. And he copied animals from picture books. One of his favorite books was called *Wild Beasts.*

Compare this picture of a zookeeper from *Wild Beasts* with Rousseau's painting.

Dream Lion

By the light of a full moon, in an imaginary desert, a woman lies fast asleep by a river. Her garment of many colors protects her from the cool night air. In her hand is a walking stick. Beside her lies her mandolin and a jug of water. A lion passing by sees her. Curious, he quietly comes closer. Ready to flee if she wakes, he delicately sniffs at her. Is he real or is he a dream? Has a lion ever visited you in your dreams?

When Rousseau painted a scary jungle scene, he sometimes got so caught up in it, he would begin to tremble with fear. To calm himself, he would run to his studio window and open it wide. The fresh Paris air helped him come back to reality from the world he was painting.

Make up a story about the sleeping musician as you add your own colors to this scene.

War

In 1893, Rousseau retired from his job at the customs house to work fulltime as an artist. To pay his bills, he gave art and music lessons to people in his neighborhood. A year later, he met the poet Alfred Jarry, who gave him the nickname *Le Douanier,* the customs official. That year, he exhibited a large painting called *War.* Rousseau painted war as an insane character riding a black horse. She holds a torch in one hand and a sword in the other. As War gallops across the landscape, she sows terror, desperation, tears, and destruction.

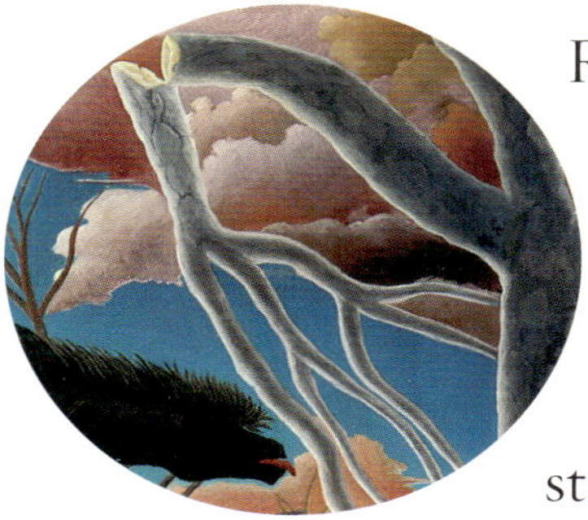

Rousseau hated war. He remembered the Franco Prussian War of 1870 in which thousands of soldiers were killed. The war also brought misery to French citizens. They could not get enough food and many starved to death.

Rousseau depicted his idea of war. Create your idea of peace.

Carnival Evening

Dressed in costume for the Carnival, a couple walks arm in arm by the light of the moon. In addition to painting, Rousseau wrote poems, plays and music, and he played the flute, mandolin and violin. He wrote music for his first wife, Clemence. After she died, he remarried. His second wife, Josephine, loved his art and exhibited his paintings in her stationery store.

Towards the end of his life, Rousseau made friends with other great artists and poets. He gave parties at his studio for his new friends. In 1908, Picasso decided to give a party for Rousseau. He wanted to honor Rousseau but ended up making fun of him, too. His famous friends occasionally played practical jokes on Rousseau and made fun at his expense, but they also admired his art.

Henri Rousseau died on September 2, 1910 in Paris, at 66 years of age. He had created a new style of art and is now celebrated as a great and original artist.

Text: Catherine de Duve
Graphic design: Philippe Plumhans
Concept and coordination: Kate'Art Editions
Translation: Wenda O'Reilly, Ph. D.

Art credits
RMN, Paris: *View of the Grenelle Bridge,* 1892: pp. 2-3 - *The Fishermen and the Biplane,* 1908: p. 2 - *Pere Juniet's Cart,* 1908: p. 2 - *Eve,* 1907: p. 3, 5, 22 - *Ship in the Storm,* after 1896: p. 3 - *Portrait of the Artist,* c. 1900-1903: p. 4 - *The Wedding Party (detail),* c. 1905: p. 8 - *The Representatives of the Foreign Powers Coming to Hail the Republic as a Token of Peace,* 1907: pp. 10, 21 - *Child with Doll,* 1904-05: pp. 12-13 - *Portrait of a Woman,* 1895: p. 13 (left) - *Portrait of Madame M.,* c. 1895-97: p. 13 (right) - *The Painter and his Wife,* 1899: p. 14 - *The Snake Charmer,* 1907: inside front cover, pp. 15, 20 - *War, or Discord on Horseback,* 1894: pp. 28-29
Photo Herve Lewansdowski/R.G. Ojeda
Beyeler Foundation, Basel: *Hungry Lion (detail),* 1905: p. 3, 24
Kunstmuseum Basel: *Forest Landscape with Setting Sun,* 1910: pp. 15, 23-25
The Samuel Courtauld Trust Institute of Art Gallery, London: *Toll Gate,* c. 1890: p. 9
The National Gallery, London: *Tiger in a Tropical Storm (Surprised!),* 1891: front cover, pp. 18-19, 21. © The National Gallery, London.
National Gallery, Prague: *Myself, Portrait-Landscape,* 1890, pp. 1, 3, 6-7
The National Gallery of Art, Washington: *Tropical Forest with Monkeys,* 1910, John Hay Whitney Collection (1982.76.7): pp. 16, 21.
The Phillips Collection, Washington: *View of the Ile Saint-Louis from the Quai Henri IV,* 1909, p. 11.
Philadelphia Museum of Art, Philadelphia: *Carnival Evening, 1886,* oil on canvas, 117 x 90 cm, The Louis E. Stern Collection (1963.181.64), p. 30.
Museum of Modern Art, New York: *The Sleeping Gypsy,* 1897: p. 26 & *The Dream,* 1910: pp. 22-23: Digital image © The Museum of Modern Art/photo SCALA, Florence.

Photographs:
The artist in front of his painting, *Jungle Landscape with Setting Sun,* 1910: p. 25 - Young jaguar with zookeeper, from *Bêtes sauvages,* c. 1900, Galeries Lafayette: p. 25 - Sheet music of Henri Rousseau's Waltz, *Clémence:* p. 31 - Rousseau and his violon & Rousseau in his studio in Rue Perrel, c. 1907: p. 31.

With thanks to: Pierre Vallaud, Director RMN, Catherine Marquet, Director of RMN publications, Marie-Dominique de Teneuille, RMN publications, Chantal Guyot and everyone who helped to make this book.

www.happymuseum.com